CELTIC HIGHWAY

CELTIC HIGHWAY

POEMS & TEXTS

Inscribed for Jolene
In admiration,
may you have A
Thousand years
of Peace!

Trevor
April, 2003.

TREVOR CAROLAN

Ekstasis Editions

National Library of Canada Cataloguing in Publication Data

Carolan, Trevor
    Celtic Highway

    Poems.
    ISBN 1-894800-09-5

    I. Title.
PS8555.A756C34 2002   C811'.54   C2002-910743-1
PR9199.3.C348C34 2002

© 2002 Trevor Carolan
Cover painting: Miles Lowry
Author photo: Julie Iverson, North Shore News

Acknowledgements:
        Thanks to the following who first published many of these poems:
*Event, Spokes, Western Living, North Shore News, Heron Press, Pearls, Arc,
Polestar Writers Daybooks, Banff Centre Press* (from *Giving Up Poetry: With Allen
Ginsberg At Hollyhock*).
        The Calgary Suite, with score by Mark Armanini, was recorded for radio
broadcast in 1990. Special thanks to soloists Michael Strutt, Erika Northcot,
and Gary Dahl. "The Blind Harper" was broadcast on American Public Radio in
1990. Many thanks to Joemy Wilson and the Carolan Consort.
        The Music of the Stones, with score by Mark Armanini, was commissioned
as a project of the Vancouver Community Arts Council in 1991. Thanks to Ingrid
Alderson, the Vancouver Chinese Classical Music Ensemble, and Sal Ferraras.

Published in 2002 by:
Ekstasis Editions Canada Ltd.   Ekstasis Editions
Box 8474, Main Postal Outlet   Box 571
Victoria, B.C. V8W 3S1   Banff, Alberta T0L 0C0

THE CANADA COUNCIL | LE CONSEIL DES ARTS
FOR THE ARTS | DU CANADA
SINCE 1957 | DEPUIS 1957

BRITISH
COLUMBIA
ARTS COUNCIL
Supported by the Province of British Columbia

Celtic Highway has been published with the assistance of a grant from the Canada
Council and the Cultural Services Branch of British Columbia.

For Patsy Carolan, Mary Carolan Hillard,
Dennis Cranmer and Bae Kil-Soo

In Memory

And for Sam Roddan, author and teacher

Irish poets, learn your trade
Sing whatever is well-made.

W.B. Yeats

CONTENTS

The Music of the Stones

Celtic Highway

Old Masters

DEEP COVE

*In the heavens at night, dark and wandering
beneath blazing Orion, flowed the starry
constellation Eridanos....*

Malcolm Lowry

It Wasn't Eve

It wasn't Eve who sinned and fell
but Adam saw her first, of course
from the corner of his eye.
Eve, cinnamon
ripe as pomegranate,
dusky-voiced,
from the confluence of the Tigris and
Euphrates.

Can you taste her now, old grandfather?
Or then, in your prime
loins jumping.

The babe that shook your bones.

SALMONBERRIES

At five o'clock we cross Cove Creek
talking baseball;
the salmonberries are a surprise.

Red succulents brighten shady thickets;
I show my son where the sweetest berries hide
ripening out of sight
beneath thick leaves.
I tell him, Tai Chi goes inside.

I'll get 'em, he says
sweetening the hazy hour
stepping forward, grasping fistfuls
with fat three-year-old hands.

We pass the time scouting ripe fruit;
spy the first tart huckleberries
on little bushes for little boys
and big ones for big dads.

All's right with the world
this early summer day
walking home together,
just the pair of us
sharing berries up Rumpelstiltskin Lane.

VESPERS, AMBLESIDE

For Kwon Tae-Jung & Nathan Strutt, in memory

At dusk the Coho leap beneath a crescent moon
in dark September waters
like forty years ago, when parents took kids upriver
to watch the big fish spawn.
We called the rocky shallows Paradise.

Tonight, the leaping salmon are my country.
At harbour, ships' beacons glimmer for love
through the haze of beachfires,
dogs dance along the shore beneath Kul-shan's gaze
south of the border;
sea-grass scrapes our shins, and the gulls cry nightfall
while the Coho leap unceasing in their vespers.

Although we talk a little among ourselves,
what new can be said of this autumn
miracle?
Look here, how the salmon forge the surging channel
as night settles and the bridge lights sparkle above
Lion's Gate.

We walk east along the trail washed umber by the moon,
the Coho leaping in silvery light,
so near we can almost touch them, reaching for perfection in
the single moment's final flight.

Only this awakening is new.
May it be forever thus, O Goddess
with the salmon dancing,
our children beside us
still knowing a world of miracles.

Simple.   Perfect.   Holy.

PRINCESS BLUEJAY

For Rose Peters, found murdered, East Vancouver, 1988

We were neighbours.
Close in a way without speaking,
nodding in silent acknowledgement
Tuesdays and Fridays
at your corner in Chinatown.

Now, running early through Cove forest,
eyes alert for movement,
I cannot pass the skunk cabbage,
its musky pungence,
the lemon bright yoni on display
and not sense your stillness.

Again I read your story on the front page;
caught in a crossfire, still a girl
taking RCMP lead in your skull in Tofino,
surviving to work the east end alleys
pumping Ritalin.

This forest home your spirit's chosen now
is all medicine,
never sees a footprint.
Cabbage season, I nod again in passing,
neckhair tingling at your uneasy presence.

Some folks'll never understand,
but we tell our kids about an Indian
princess who came to live with the bluejays,
taking their name, becoming this place.

This is what sacred is;
it becomes what sacred means
when we teach our children
why we bow.

GATHA ON CLEANING FISH

Cleaning fish with Harabuji
we offer thanks,
scraping scales:
a bucket of gleaming cod from
Skookumchuck Narrows.

Grandpa scrapes, snips fins and spines,
slits belly from vent to gills.
Poking, I grab the guts,
yank and trim with my blade.

God of the Rockfish, many thanks;
God of the Dogfish, forgive us:
Yer critters are hard to eat.

Through these cod we return again to sea,
as sea becomes our flesh.
All one again
through the cruel hook.

THE CHESTNUT JUNCO

Last night, Christmas—
The wind took out powerlines;
we rocked the kids asleep in blankets,
read for hours by candlelight
and rose with sunlight flooding the world.

Our Jesus-bread on the front porch
drew jays and flickers,
grey sou-westers driving them back to cover.
Later, Jizo, Buddha of children and travellers
looked up through falling snow
and sent the junco.

The children knew him:
a rare bird, chestnut flanks rouged with winter.
The snowy world stood still;
and for a moment I saw
the master's hand in old Kyoto:
Red Forest-Tit On Snow Bamboo.
What was that old Zen painter's name?

I know, hollers the youngest:
We'll call him *Gassho*!

* *Gassho*: a term of respectful thanks used among Japanese Buddhists

$3,000 Haiku

Big Rudi's back from his Celtic tramp
through Scotland;
Just a sentimental journey, shank's mare
Iona to Holy Isle.

T'was alright, says he;
a good holiday:
no more, no less.
Fine weather, good company,
blisters the size of Loonies;
Twelve days upon the open road
in old monk's habit:

No enlightenment.

Tried it all, says he.
Meditation, reading Basho,
staying mindful
up hill, down dale.
What old Alcuin
must have seen and thought
on his own great walk
to Charlemagne
I'll never know.

Truly, no sudden awakening.
Just this haiku of sorts:
      Morning after night rain
      Dew glistens like pearls strung on sheep wire.
      Purple thistles bark, Fare well!

BIG WHISKERS AND THE GREAT TAO

Socked in,
October fog shrouds the Cove.
In the foreground, only a few boats and shacks
up Indian Arm still visible.

Yet, special this: the stray, dull cry of glaucous gulls
and buffleheads that paddle silent at the edge of the mist,
where bull-kelp and logging slash float aimless on the great Tao
like an image from Ma-Yuan.

Along the shore, I move slowly,
shaking out cobwebs in reluctant exercise.
Suddenly, a dark figure cuts the surface:
ah, Big Whiskers, kid's book bestseller
and harbour seal extraordinaire,
clean head cruising like a tomahawk missile.
He's back from summer!

Track closely with your eye the white furl of his wake
as he swells and arcs in the fog,
cruising the shallows and rising a mighty black moment
like Big Daddy Orca
or Magic Johnson driving straight to the hoop.

Listen to the echo, loud as gunshot,
his flippers smacking the bay in pure devilment,
ploughing the sargasso
without shortcut, without stopping
when he dives, like the green dot at sunset,
a blip and gone.

How did the old monk describe it?
A sauve young frog by his pond,
Kersplosh!
Silence once more?
How the old song goes on;
this life's worth having after all.

WEEP WILLOW

For Larry Lillo, in memory

The baby laughing, saw you first;
the new roof next door had caught my eye.
I didn't recognize you.

God, he's changed; gaunt, the cane.
Elegant almost, moving slow.

You'd had the sun, nutbrown;
then the rime of sweat,
cream flecked beside your nose:
The sickness.

Good to see the sun back, I nodded.
It hasn't rained long, really, you said.
It's like Hawaii here, the flowers and vines
Colour everywhere…
This is the most beautiful city in the country.

Our eyes locked up close: he's dying, I saw.
No aid for it.
It's our apple tree I'm worried about—
She blossomed with the warm, I said.
And the hail's been pounding;
we took a course, to get the pruning right.
She's a pagoda now; let's hope the bees
are working…
It'll be alright, you smiled, weary with
climbing stairs.

We stood clairvoyant, the three of us
under a healing sun
beside the Cove.
We prune ours too, you said pointing upward.
That weeping willow.
The baby waved her shoe.

O Willow weep. Weep for grief, for art, lost youth.
Weep willow; do not weep soft.

Then friends arrived;
Surprise in the air.
We talked as locals,
the others moving about their business.
I said, I've read this fellow in *The Guardian*;
He writes,
　　Nothing wrong with magic realism
　　But it's real magic we're needing now....

Then a quick spring chill blew down from the snowline.
Your lowered head, that gap-toothed smile;
the whole blessed bay sparkled 'round us
and the willow rocked above in April breeze
with the sound of your cane, its tapping;
the numbering of days.
And so we walked along.

O Willow weep; weep soft.
Weep willow, and do not spare our tears.

MUSHROOM HUNTING

Mushroom hunting with Bear in a drizzle
above the Cove,
an old line from the past chants up through
forest duff:

> The master's gone away
> herb-picking on the mount
> cloudhidden, whereabouts unknown

You know how it goes;
kicking around the undergrowth
tramping in boots, dog sniffing out fresh
'shrooms for Dad.
Mind empty,
bag swelling steadily with the fresh boletus,
Heart Sutra beating time:
Gate gate paragate parasamgate bodhi svaha.

Peeking through thorn burrs, there's the Cove—
calm today in grey November: Hey, dog,
the rain's stopped!
Bear trots over, pleased to demonstrate
the keenness of her truffle-pig nose.

Searching deep in her eyes;
is that transcendental contact?
Does a dog have the Buddha-nature?
Just nod yes or no, I urge her quietly,
secretly waiting enlightenment.
No answer:
The young bitch just wants to play.

THE DOLLARTON VARIATIONS

Malcolm Lowry, squatter,
  Dollarton: 1939-53

Lowry walked here;
Dee Livesay, Earle Birney too,
where Weston and Varley came to paint these
Pacific waters lapping at the shore.

Not much has changed.
It's still cougar wild;
towhees work the cover of vine-maple and salal.
These hemlocks knew Lowry's scent, the skunky tang on
inlet freshets, calm as the ice-age.

Sheltered in barnacle rockery where he swam,
a silent heron wades and a cormorant wings east.
Thirty paces from Malcolm's patch, a two-inch salmon fry
undulates the shifting tide:
Beware, beware the gulls and smoky grebes.

Arrested by an intruder's presence, mating squirrels dart
past memory rock where he lived.
Even the ghosts have left this place;
not a scrap of charcoal remains from the squatters'
shacks that District workers finally torched.

Let the humping squirrels mock us;
so much life here still,
beyond the range of wireless communication under
the volcano,
or above the gin grave he knew too well.

THE MIST IN THE GLEN

The mist hangs in the trees;
late February sun radiant
through fishscale clouds;
salal glistening after night rain.

Walking through the grove
south of our mushroom trail,
meditating on Deng Zhou-ping's death in China
I remark on last night's Council skirmish here
that took no prisoners either.

Some things, Churchill knew—
No surrender.

Parkside Creek rushes on and on.

SHOVELLING DUNG

Waiting on the manure truck
we sit round the kitchen with our boots on,
chewing muffins, drinking coffee.
Then, honk! Grinding gears, a squeal of
air brake at the fence.

Two fellas tromp up back of the dumper,
sink to their shins as she angles steep,
squawking with hydraulic thrust.
Her tailgate flaps like a giant anus
dropping a steaming load on the blacktop:
Three rich yards of golden dung,
heaved up ripe from delta cowbarns
sweating in late morning sun.

Out with the shovels;
pay off the boys and commence pitching that
load over top the fence:
Ten bucks a cubic yard—believe the geezer
who says, *Where there's muck, there's money.*

A pitching shovel heaves cowshit up and over
the backyard fence,
spreads it thin and even over the earth.
A digging spade, long-handled gets them
hard-to-reach corners.
My sweetie strides on by in red Wellies.
"Don't go getting fancy fella," she says;
"We gotta rake it out later anyways."

Kids walking by pretend not to notice.
My wife returns with the coffee
saying, "Wow, what a stink!
How can you stand it!
Old folks out to market, stop to chat
flowers, and pickles, and bulbs.
"Yup, she looked fine last year, yer garden;
like a little bit of heaven here in all
these buildings… Mind yer back now."

And there she is:
A sunny, vegetable garden,
five months of summer eating
and hardy greens the winter through.
A little elbow grease and a sporty
cowshit topcoat keeps it fighting trim.

The Indian kid in leather who never says a word,
comes by, the pile getting smaller.
"Man, that's right," he barks. "We need that
stuff 'round here… Put a little country
back in this here town."

You betcha.

Then we load up buckets and dump 'em round
poplars and boxwood,
on grape vines and shrubs,
on burdock for medicine,
packed loose 'round berries and laurels,
bamboo and thorn-hedge, lilac and honeysuckle,
on fruit trees, the tulips:
The sweet dung smell fills the neighborhood.

A good morning's work.
A decent sweat worked up better 'n sit-ups,
and for days thereafter
the rich barnyard perfume
fills yer nose like a sonnet stolen straight from the Muse.
Ah, springtime!

THE CALGARY SUITE

In the wake of desire, certain facts came hounding.

Fred Stenson

CORTES MEDITATION

Sunrise:
first morning breath,
cabin in north island forest
curtains drawn open:
outside
pine boughs bathed in amber
cathedral light.

"JACKSON'S RANCH, CACHE CREEK, 1948"

This image speaks.
A Cariboo ranch tamed among dry hills.
The plateau lands are like this,
peaceful as wavering poplars
trim as grazing mares;
an old song in magenta and lime-green.

His trigonometry is correct.
The world is weathered as the angles of
these rough exteriors;
as textured as this shaded palette
that draws us straightforth unto
night.

MEDITATION II: CALGARY

This year no autumn.
Merely an exchange of climatic
polarities:

Summer/Winter.
A blink in transition.
Snow

in September.

CHINOOK

The snows have melted on Prince Island.
Canvasbacks mottle the beaver marsh.
The stepping stones across the creek are
wet again
and the secrets I meant to tell you
are now immaterial.
Whispers are better graced with
patience;
snow will fall again.

Along the river pathways
the marsh is alive with sound this
November Saturday,
the dull world wakened.

Beneath the swing bridge over the Bow
two young lovers
tousled by the shore;
I watched them with a scholar's smile;

Walked on,
humming an old melody for hours.

MADONNA AND CHILD

They breathe soft within the folds
of heavy winter quilts,
prairie light diffused above them
on simple walls.
Babe, bare-legged, all milky curves
crooked in mother's arms,
each asleep beyond fatigue,
beyond the world.

Holy pictures were something like this.

The child tosses;
mother nestles closer in sleep.
There are no words.

The sun climbs above bare January trees.

BREAKUP

The Bow's swift currents gnash and snap
these cubist shags of pack ice.
Grinding subterranean teeth
crush them crazily ashore:
a Western ode to spring thaw.

Yesterday, muddy tracks on morning ice.
A river mink slithered to the current,
froze mid-scamper at my gaze,
a snatch of jet against the white.
She looked up, nervous at my smile,
disappearing in melt-water.

The March sun beams;
the Bow's winter membrane has grown filthy.
Time to go.
My heart pierces to the core.

A square white sun.
Clouds lazy as innuendos curling the sky.
Time to go.

Time to go.

An October Walk Along The Bow

Would Thomas Merton notice these mallards
in migrant plumage,
or the gull, white-breasted in unexpected
pleasure of a late sun?

This river flows dangerously sudden
with a rush of glaciers in its eddies,
chilled with the nearness of mountain ice.
Its colours are its own
or of rolling skies that quicken step and breath
above the lightning rods of Calgary's petro-towers.

Poetry here is all in the land
in awkward prairie ways that linger
like the leaves of mountain ash
along the runoff slopes
here, now.
As I walk homeward, upstream
without invitation
or desire.

Meditation III

This is how we learn new places
in the heart:

Hunting apartments in all day rain,
blistered in boots,
weighing the kindness
in strangers' faces.

Above the boulevards, poplars weave
in evening light;
winter aching into numbness.

With a sigh
the yearning comes;
a thousand mirror shards
exploding in darkness.

OSCILLATION

Metaphor;
we looked for metaphor,
for ways of explanation;
got hooked on one poor word:
Resentment.

But I want to tell you now
It's time to open the door
and let the healing in.
You know this:
That in the heart there lies a cruelty
beyond language.

I bring these words with the hunger
of a wave-tossed man;
this oscillation at my centre
anaesthetizes language.

There are no words.
No metaphors
for this thing we cannot express in words
while the moon wanes.

BODY ENGLISH

We know this:
our lover walks upon the ground,
the land before us is the lotus land.

But our November kisses,
and the hardness of your form
inspire choruses in blue-green prairie dusk.
The glory of love, did you say?
Glory indeed, this commonplace office,
another pair of darkened beasts
embracing beneath dewy
street-lamps in blackening snow:

A Year for Living Dangerously.

THE MUSIC OF THE STONES

It's getting hard to be someone, but it all works out

John Lennon

THE MUSIC OF THE STONES

This is the story of a wounded man,
a pilgrim and a garden,
a still place; fifteen stones dry
as the driest places of the heart.
And of earth, healing dew
the inner spring.

McJazz sat three hours before raked,
bleached rock.
Journey ended, home.
He breathed again:
stones and water
moss and pine.
The sleepy drone of bees beyond the wall
suggested firmament, an epiphany
beyond the shabby patina
of this dusty world.

Breathe.
Just breathe.

These reconciliations of the heart,
of love, of wanting mind:
we move toward them in our fashion,
marking stations along the way,
finding quietude, at last
in the nexus temporal and eternal:
In the music of these stones
existing in time
Mindfully. Timelessly.

Breathe.
Just breathe.

In Nepal

Down from Pokhara,
from the snows of Machhapuchare
descending valleys
into Katmandu on a rubberneck bus,
we stop a moment
in some nameless village,
taking on passengers
for the final run to town.

Before us, outside the window,
dragged barefoot in chains
through the dust,
in wild-eyed horror
or lunacy, we cannot know;
trousers, shirt, hair violently askew,
some luckless peasant thrashes out his soul,
ears gleaming red in terror.

Brutality is powerful theatre;
we gasp our speculation at his crime.
Murder? Or some new injustice on the meek:
what special madness in this parched terrain?

O Kumari, they tell us mind our place;
this is no land for heroes.
Policemen here invent the law.
Fearing the worst, we understand at last what
Conrad knew:

　　The Heart of Darkness.

Here, in the Himalayas,
God's dust embraces us once more
upon the winding road
to Katmandu.

THE RUINS AT PAGAN

The Irrawaddy plains are reddened
by a thousand arid years of secrets;
the builders of these crumbling monuments
unknown.

In the hundreds, by the thousands
these temples annoint Pagan,
no Ozymandias, no clue
to the silence which is their history,
unknowable as the dry, eroding wind.

Still early morning,
our pony cart jogs up a dusty track
as Kublai Khan must once have done.
We pass the riddles,
the lesser temples,
entering Thatbyinnyu, climbing stairs
to gaze across a vista
no archaeologist ever knew.
In wind as fine as rosin
these red-bricks echo louder than the
slash of Mongol time.

The shapeless peanut fields
triumphed at Pagan;
now rough ponies lead pilgrims
to the Buddha's sacred footprints.
And men who once enslaved the Thai
hawk trinkets, mostly fake,
to scattered tourists in the dust
in the ruins of the golden city
at Pagan.

GOLDEN MONASTERY, MANDALAY

Chancing on the temple in our fatigue
we enter through bamboo and iron trees
where pie-dogs eye us,
too hot to bark.

The monks' huts circle a tidy compound;
laughter rings loud around the bath-jar
where robes awry
a novice boy escapes a dousing,
sending chickens fleeing through the scrub.

Our arrival is unexpected.

We tread up worn teak stairs,
the temple raised aloft above the floods
or God knows what,
and stroke its hand-sawn beams
amber with time.

Feet scuff bare upon the planks,
creak clock-wise around the veranda.
Chickens scratch beneath pillars
on the ground.
Foundations settled in decay,
wall panels wobbling at a finger's touch.

Within,
shards of light pierce heavy, incensed air;
the Buddha image sits in shadow,
We bow, mindfully.

In a corner,
old crones gathered around him
before the Buddha image,
the abbot chuckles from his chair.

Time for reflection:
Ego, ergo bellum.

This could be no other place but Mandalay;
no sounds but the sounds of the world
without,
the pad of feet upon the stairs.

Shaped by the road,
we tend to our devotions
and sit awhile before the altar
in pleasant gloom
without expense, or second thought

Safe within the Triple Gems
of family, this garden Earth, and our holy Lord,
the Healing Buddha

the World Awakened One.

DARUMA

How often I dreamed of this great
opportunity.
Living alone
in silence
with time to natter at my aches
or stretch my limbs,
working odd hours as I please.

A sheepskin wrap keeps out the damp,
and sleeping late until nine or even ten
is sweeter than a juicy peach.

I crave conversation from time to time;
but when it comes,
enough is soon enough.
Being alone gets us down to serious business:

That's why Daruma
came from out of the west.

MORNING PRAYER

Sun buddhas,
buddhas of the Moon,
of the mountains, the forest
the waters,
of the trees, the plants, flowers.

O Buddha of the morning star and
heavens

Hear me

Grant us health,
more kindness,
your patience,

And compassion.

TAI CHI LIFE

Time past is past.
The continuum, irretrievable;
the garden paradise forever gone
yet never irredeemable:

Heaven binds the cosmos with ineluctable order,
else all our masterworks of hand, arts, science
are nothing more than fisheyes.

There is a grace in discipline.

In the absence of birds one hears other sounds,
drifting leaves
rippling water.
Beneath a wooden bridge lay carp suspended
among the ornamental stones of a pond.

A hillside garden.
Among the rocks above a curl of river a solitary figure
weaves patterns in the dawn,
sweeps low, rises

Golden Pheasant Greets The Sun.

Each day
this subtle art
stilling the infernal chatter of the mind,
the way of change,
self-forgetfulness,
movement within stillness:

Carry the Tiger.

Return to Mountain.

The Earth breathes for us.
Her seasons cast their separate breaths upon
the lake;
what we are to know, perhaps is known
the rest is merely hunger

Step Back, Repulse the Monkey.

Hours.
The heron waits motionless in shadow,
neither of, nor not of transformation
along the shore.

Figures dance at daybreak among the rocks
like music, threading light.

White Stork Cools His Wings.

Silence has no language;
no words for stillness
Only this:
Each day, mindful practice:
Image without sound
Content within form.

Ride the Tiger.

Return to Mountain.

PRACTICE

Practice and practice to be faithful
the way a blacksmith forges iron,
hammer and hammer
for truth and falsehood have no
difference in time:
today, Prime Minister;
tomorrow, nothing.
Truly, true can be false;
truly, false can be true.
And things are not always
what they seem to be.

SATORI, LONSDALE AVENUE

The Lions glower back of Lonsdale hilltop.
Westerly freshets fill my lungs and brain.
Drunk on perfumed air, in mid-day garden,
bursting with joy, I read the signs:

Maples afire, tulips fading, blue-bells
dancing in the shade.
Swathed in light, clouds gathering behind,
I sing out
and don't mind who's listening,

What a beautiful world!

The flowers in bloom as I glance from
my room,
and the west wind blowing clean, tell me
I'd rather stroll here, in sight of the sea
than lunch at Elaine's even with the Gypsy Kings.

My jewels are this light:
these pathways,
the lion pillars of the North Shore peaks.

This beauty is my offering
to life, joy
to compassion!

And the ferry cast off from the Quay,
its waking foam, plume of gulls
is my Aloha and Mahalo to the spirits of
this place above the harbour.

Blues-time is all blue skies now;
it's satori on the sunny side of the street,
with sou'westers winking in from Point Grey
bluffs:

Clear skies ahead
More light

And so, each day passes.

GATHERING STONES

...a time for gathering stones together

Ecclesiastes

WHISKEY JAZZ

     I. Black 'n Blues

Ben Webster had bad feet.
Played big 'n sweet on tenor sax.
Big Ben Webster blowing Paris blues
all over the eaves and glistening flagstones,
being Basie bad.

Them teenage dreams we never shake
they rattle us for years
like blue lights on a darkened stage:
old berets and leather jackets,
old loves and old lies
like the gal you loved so bad,
that got away.

Bad Ben would have known what to do
He wouldn't gamble on no lucky horseshoe
or no silver dollar;
he'd grab them blues you got by the neck so hard
Baby, that riff'd make your head spin.

But them feets. Can't get 'em outa my mind;
Old man Jack the dicer told me 'bout them feet
and seems like nothing's been the same since then:
A giant-killer wi' his dogs gone bad.

It's never a hero comes round when we need 'em;
Always trouble to settle up on our own;
Never an easy chair when you want one
Never a jelly roll when you got the taste.

II. *Lovin' Ashes*

Yep, another one them loves gone bad.
Them belladonna eyes, 'n all that Billie Holiday
Lover man yak.

Whoa they sting, them loves gone bad,
roaming out late
then home with the sniff of innocence around
the collar
and a cheesy smile.

But we hang on, don't let go this time.

Yeah, I seen my house laid low in ashes
like dust down to the ground
rawed up again in the woe of the lost lands.

You tell me you so lucky in love;
Just beware them two-by-fours 'round every corner.

III. *This Bud's For You*

Woke after sweetsome all-night dreams,
Son House death letter blues
rockin' my skullbone through the
wee-est hours.

Woke to find the roof still leaking,
falling through
or is it just the ground that's sinking?

Call it karma, call it dues time;
it's hard to say why the blues come down:
but I know now
why Gauguin just upped and ran away.

IV. *Let's Stay Home*

Let's stay home all day
and make love slow
with rain outside,
and kids below
Sleepy Girl, round in every proper place.

Let's drink coffee
read Kerouac's golden promises
run baths,
knock around the November rugs.
We can eat what's there;
no need to go outside in the world.

Let's stay home all day
and make love slow
same like last night,
hot as high school,
succulent as the moon.
Sticky universe.

LEONARD PELTIER

Leonard, when you saluted in the squad-car
struggling with the Mounties as they sped you off in chains
we saw then the fix was in.

Did your skin recoil at the ermine robes
and velvet of our justice hall?
Your yankee government called you Murderer,
reaching across our feeble border for your scalp.

In a Vancouver courthouse, your fate hung by a thread
sustained by no more than the chanting of those Salish brothers,
and the rhythm of the medicine drums.
Our porcine minister dispensed an efficacious justice:
Return him.
And in the keening of the old ones
I heard the wailing of captive Jews led into Babylon.

Our nation-verdict surprised no one,
but we who needed most to believe
in justice: mothers, fathers, working folk,
we thought we had the day for once.
And I still see you, standing proud
the stench of rough-justice lingering where we last saw you
fighting in the squad car with the goons,
shackled and cramped amid the alien corn,
led off to solitary.

Leonard, handed over to a dark cell
in North Dakota,
had you already commenced
the marking off of days and years,
in hibernation hidden from the sun?

VETERAN'S HOSPITAL BLUES

October:
Alphonse sits alone all day
mute as granite,
hard as prairie water.
The land still lies vast
before his eyes:
memories of summer grain, harvest-time
women fat with child
banked in his pockets.

The old Ukrainians are the craziest ones
sitting about all day,
pacing endless corridors
mumbling in half-remembered tongues
of lives worked out,
and of saddle ponies still tied up
at the granary near Lvòv.

November:
Oldtimers sit around morning sofas
beneath wallpaper trees,
full of breakfast, flipping magazines.
Alphonse blinks.
Doc Horsfeld scratches his nose.
Benches creak with the chewing of
old men's cud.
Anton the Pole, moustache stiff and starched
stares out the polished windows.
Doc says, them there trees now;
my, they're getting old...
(Old men, mossy, still as hemlock.)

Today is Monday, November 14.
Doc scratches his nose beneath the calendar,
the clock ticks quiet in our mumbling retreat.
Outside, a yearling buck darts clear across
the lawn.

December:
Christmas everybody! Christmas soon!
No one bats an eye.
Billy London bums smokes from his nurse.
Matt Carelli has no brandy.
Tony Fado wants a girl.
Harry Finley says it's all gone crazy now,
'n he ought to know.
Love tunes drift from the radio.

Big Matt hobbles in for a leak
Billy L sings like a bullfrog to his own
new tune,
and Wendy the tea-girl, singing as always:
"Over and over, I keep going over
the world we knew…"

HERPES

Sometimes I almost love you
demon
when there's nothing left but yet more grief
or resignation,
the women mad again or painfully kind
at forced apartness,
dreaming of yet another innovative
pas de deux.

You don't hurt much anymore, it's true;
a blister or two, a touch of fever,
the grace of fifteen years sufferance.
They say I'm a veteran at the clinic
a real specimen,
signing me up for every new study:
modest expenses for long marchers nowadays,
if you please.

Noblesse oblige.
You're a part of me, there's no denying it
tucked away in my lower vertebrae,
in all your cauliflower glory
coming to grind away another week.
It seems I've got to love you in the old-fashioned way
as a man loves a woman, for better or worse
ashes to ashes
'til death do us part.

SEPARATISM

For Vincent Varga

That time we cruised to Edmonton
in the company car,
remember?
Riding through separatist country
jamming on the radio, rocking our blues
right up that yellow brick road.

Ain't ignorance bliss?
We had our tigers by the tail, for sure.
The steers grazed mellow by the treeline.
But here's the inside dope:
one day it's cherry pie
the next, yer rinsed and minced.

Hey, the radio!
Rock Me Baby, remember?

Hear yer fingers thinking...

Four Brief Glimpses Of Eternity

I. *Eightfold Path*

Sometimes the weariness takes over:
I'll never make the next dharma class.

We drag ourselves along,
practice with heavy bodies
going slow.

We're there, keeping time;
others drift astray, lost in the world.
Who's to keep the lantern burning?

There's nectar even in weary practice,
in fatigue;
rowing the dharma boat
to farther shores.

II. *Diamond Teachers*

Hui-Neng heard
Diamond Sutra, Third Section.
Got realization, he said.
Jack Kerouac heard *Diamond Sutra*.
"I'm thru playing the American.
Now I'm gonna live a quiet life."
Got realization, he said.

Woke up. World looked like hell.
Mist rising up inlet,
up mountain.
Got realization.
No, it's heaven I see, I said:
eight days 'til Christmas.

III. *Awareness-Practice Poetics*

Correct posture.
Notice girls' bums.
Ginsberg looking like old Bodhidharma in the mountains:
oughta do this everyday for slouching back/
bad posture.
Morning, early; still dark?
Look at other people's posture, aching backs—
Probably he's taught meditation in the West to more people
than the Dalai Lama, or anyone.
Four minutes up already.

IV. *Sifu Explains the Reverse Punch*

This is what he says:

Talk about it all you like
but sooner or later
you've got to practice.

In engineering, first year students
learn the whole big bridge;
in fifth year, the bridge
in one inch sections.

ON THE PARTING OF AN OLD FRIEND

Your road leads off to the void
and already I think of your dispatches.
Look at the pair of us
drunk again
too old now, or rather,
not old enough to grieve
else it seem unseemly.

May your destination be fertile
and your labour worthy of reward.
And of begrudgers, as the prophet truly writes,
    They Have Had Their Reward.

Let stale office moulder other envoys, Attila.
Remember always;
we are bound for the same final teahouse.

CONSANGUINITY: MONODRAMA
AFTER SIMONE SIGNORET

I.

There is a face in the mirror
and you do not know if it can be trusted:
Caravaggio.
The expression perhaps, may have everything
to do with love
or nothing:
    Green eye ...

The pain is hardly temporary;
the ache of weeks rekindled by a chance remark,
and the whiskey is back in the kitchen:
the emptiness is here to stay.
We recognize it instinctively
like the far-off walk of an old friend.

Beyond the window one figure dominates,
walking clothes, tweeds, old boots,
tramping the riverbank,
river frozen, a single sheet of ice.

It is not that we are able to cope with our pain
but that we must.

II.

Recall a tiresome evening in a cafe
sitting alone for hours,
How do we come to be there
when the glow of company, the certainty of night
might resonate instead?

Our lover asks for prayer beads
and speaks of the books they are reading at school:
Genocide a required text.

But the wheel is sure; the pain will lessen.
Your lover asks you for a portrait,
yet consider the camera's exacting eye:
does the lens move within?
Let us speculate on the power of image,
when image becomes symbol.

But, what would you say to all of this,
of grief, time, washed like gravel over a creekbed,
flowing, grinding?
Perhaps you would say nothing.
The Japanese say nothing.

III.

Snapshot: another occasion
the end of a difficult evening, no sleep.
A late night call, then disappointment.
What is it about these knocking syncopations
the unexpected conversations and amber wine;
do we sense fatal invitation?
Or are these things of no importance whatsoever,
exisiting as amazements only
like ballerinas in tights of a Saturday morning class,
swivelling
delighting in that first transcendent moment of God's grace?

Your lover speaks of discipline, but to what
purpose? The dancer's form, erectness
is present without contradiction in your pleasure.
Your lover wants a mentor
and prayer beads.

      IV.

Beyond the window, Elk country
Beaver, mink, otter, redwings, orioles:

Your lover speaks of darkness;
darkness and the edge,
the cry of the anchor for the heart
the womb of night,
the passions spent.

What I would whisper to you now is that love comes
dearest in its calmest form,
or else throw these things away as men have done
since time began,
smashed to atoms; linked only by a single need.

Think of that strange seed
the random chaos of the universe
that enters in an unexpected hour wreaking havoc:
our small cruelties to each other
the clash of yin and yang.

It is time to speak of healing.
Healing. The wounds are deep, the scars still
fresh in mind.

Searching for omens we find them everywhere;
yet in this instance,
no warning.
A flicker in the corner of the mirror perhaps,
some lack of resolution, a faltering
then, the void.

The price we pay for enlightenment.

      V.

You spoke of passion
the late night calls,
"I have to see you!"

The strawberries and beaujolais you set,
Kertesz on your night-table.

Snapshot: the lovers drawing unto night.
Cries from the neighbours up the airshaft.

The rain washes away interpretation.

CELTIC HIGHWAY

Down down the glen
Rode the bold Fenian men…

HONOLULU

Leaving the bar
we walk along Wai Canal.

Hawaiian midnight,
the hum of traffic, blue breeze behind
us.

Stopping along the railings,
she scratches my back.
The tide ebbs imperceptibly
at our embrace.

NIGHT SONGS OF THE RIVER HERON

Night in the tropics
crickets rub before the rain.

Caw!
Night heron swoops the reedy creek
running out to Hilo Bay.
A blur in the shadows;
one brief white splash,
then darkness again.

Sudden patter of rain on elephant ear,
Listen…

PRAIRIE TOWNS

Not much romance in strange towns,
rooms casting lamplight
on shallow streets
driving us out of doors
hips throbbing with loneliness.

Prairie towns are all love and hate,
new-fallen snow crisp underfoot.
Come winter though
there's something beautiful
about thirty below:
the unvarnished sounds of truth,
poplars exploding;
shifting, snapping river ice
half-buffalo men, raw as frostbitten peckers.

When we were kids, we slept out
summers in the thorn patch,
staring overhead at Telstar
needling through the heavens
or so it seemed.

Tonight, after five and a half hours
in Bronco Billy's
we head for the Bow to catch the
moonlight on the river shallows,
pissing by the rail-bridge, looking up
at the vision overhead.

Not much has changed
in Prairie town;
the love and hate linger on
like greasy spoons in Winnipeg, '57.
Not much romance in these here rooms
we try and make a home,
when home's so far away
the stars above begin to look like
neighbours.

MORNING DANCE ABOVE FORT SAN

Soft as cottonwood,
heels test firmament in stony furze
above Fort San,
eyes drawn to a distant church by the lake
stark against the ochre palette
of deep Saskatchewan
like Tuscany, or the Okanagan.

Below, the lodge hums loud with words.
Blackbird sings his matins,
flashing ruddy chevrons;
underfoot, harsh erosion gullies
beg mindfulness.

These hills have seen it all:
weather grounding movement,
gravity the mother of light in a landscape
two-thirds sky,
clouds merely requia between larger stanzas.

Ahead, canola flows to the very margins of Oz.
A grasshopper melds with his bracken
and vanishes momentarily,
sensing other means through rough terrain.

This gorse, clumped and awkward underfoot
might lend itself to festive dancing,
but Heron's dance is all concealed articulation,
the counterweight of bone on fossil bone.
Avoid the prickly pear.
The Buddha's Seven Star Step reverses poles,
ju-jitsus east to west
south to north,
all the same.

O'Nami, the truly Great
before his final victory
sat *zazen* all night in worry
until his master revealed
the secret of the ocean wave,
its stillness unstoppable,
flowing weight,
as the sacred dance above the lake
bespoke the silence of the wind.

Mare's tails waver along the road;
the sky breaks up at noon.
Jangling through the berries
an olive-skinned woman steps lightly
up the Fort's healing trail
collecting fronds.

There!

Grasshopper leaps,
a glint amid wild medicine
'n vanishes.

Fort Qu'Appelle
Saskatchewan

STARRY NIGHT, BIG SUR

Biggest Big Dipper anyone ever saw
that starry night; brighter'n a drive-in movie,
juniper and shore-pine snapping on the fire.

Our kids drift off with mom's stories
as comets fall like neon overhead,
August's healing breeze dressing up the southern cliffs
under Leo.

Henry Miller wrote this coast;
Kerouac sat at Bixby Canyon going mad.
We forage for tinder with our kids,
meet strangers at the campground
like back in the old days before The Fall.

O tender harmonicas of night,
the pines sway to your blue flamenco.
Twelve hundred miles from home
Jeffers and Everson lullaby us in the wine dark night.

The embers glow; our sooty kettle boils,
we crack the spirits and stare deep into the mystery.

On the trail for poetry
On the road for love
So far from home
So far to go.

Shooting stars
Lost in the ocean of night,
Big Sur *gloria*
O *tempus magisterium*!

Lost Hills, East of Bakersfield

Santana wind:
dust, dust blowing everywhere
in gray lost hills:
Chapparal, manzanita, sage,
yucca, spikey palm.
Even desert birds are drab.

The migrant workers live in tents
beside us in the camping grounds;
Wardrobes, extension cords poke through
the door flaps,
Yip-yip of television glows in the
gortex sheath of home.
Bikes, cats, boxes, and drums piled here
and there. Mexicans.

Desert dusk, slate red.
Last night's sky turned violet
before the dimming and Santana blow;
we lashed our poles for safety
beneath Venus, the first bright star,
pointing to the Milky Way down south.

I took a leak with the drifters
on the edge of the sagelands.
'Round here, this kinda blow
ain't nothing yet, one said.
And there above us, with kids sleeping nearby,
the rich harvest of the heavens glittered
like tiny silver apples of the moon

FOR ALL THE TEA IN CHINA
Journeys in the Middle Kingdom

> *There's something akin between the Irish and the Chinese.*
> *I don't know... Something impractical.*
> Xiao Qian

TRAVELLING 3RD CLASS, HARD-SEAT, AMONG THE MASSES
Canton – Guilin line, 1985

I.

Riding Third Class, Hard-Seat, among the masses is not for the
squeamish.
From Canton by rail, tickets gained after day-long
red-tape torment,
endless queues,
impenetrable bureaucratic logic:
Ad astra per aspera, we learn our Hong Kong agent has picked our
pockets smartly.

Fortune in great measure!
From a Japanese long-hair we learn yin/yang of black market money
exchange,
buy our tickets with hot renminbi at half official tourist rate.

Money-changing in the workers' square is not for the faint of heart:
ten thousand pairs of eyes.
We dodge the militia
mill among throngs, observe them, turn back their glances
en passant.

The station plaza heaves with humanity in the March chill:
rumpled army fatigues, Mao caps everywhere,
but ragtag Western threads are in surprising number.

II.

Our soup is scalding—pork dumplings and scallions—best tucker
for the ride ahead.
The open-air kitchen sweats green grease;
numb with cold, skies dim and grey,
we huddle about its vats of bubbling onion broth.

Canton station is well-provisioned:
wayfarer's biscuits, shell nuts, dry fruit, rice sweets—acres of grub
unfathomable to Sai-yan.
Heroic Station of the Masses! O Stalinist heap of brick and plaster,
dull as prairie winter!

All Aboard!

A rabid crush erases our aesthetics

All Aboard!
Entry gates thrown open, crowd runs amok, tramples the weakest
underfoot:
Third Class, Hard-Seat is not for the lily-livered.
First come, first served.
That's all.

III.

You've seen it all before—Doctor Zhivago,
huddled masses, Goya's frantic peasants;
carriage aisles awash in baggage,
a sea of fleshy peasant denim.
No scrap of Middle Kingdom splendour here;
no Buddha, no precious jade among these Third Class, Hard Seat
wayfarers.

And no sleeping berths.
But there are seats to sit on, more or less
and we are thankful, believe it: standing all the way to Guilin town,
a day, maybe two, is not unthinkable. Many do,
crushing us with errant shoulders, knobby knees and bags.
    Whoaaa!!!
              All Aboard!

Blizzards of steam outside the windows;
a swaying, jerking throb of humanity—Dr. Zhivago help!

Spitting cinders blacken the world.
Floorboards shudder violently beneath us,
the People's locomotive cranks down the line;
by god, the damned thing leaves on time.

     IV.

Snapshot: three humans cramped in every seat for two,
cluttered as bag ladies,
choking on blue air.

Every Male Must Smoke, surely a Party decree;
all puffing amiably, coughing down each other's necks.

Consciousness is low among the masses.

But our seats in fact are not so hard;
merely stiff, protestant;
like Mrs. Arbuckle's proper Yorkshire parlour.

(Snapshot: Mrs. A. sat here beside us, squashed elegantly among
Third Class, Hard-Seat travellers, cheerfully drinking tea.
Rock On, Step Steady Ladies!)

Our humming carriage rocks down the line packed to Third World bursting;
aisles plugged tight, country louts a-braying in each other's ears:
workers off to the capital, aunties off to Shanghai, Nan-ling.
God be thanked, our ride is short—
thirty-six hours only.

Twenty minutes out of Canton
the air is Blue, stinking,
Unbreathable:

Can we last?

V.

We've donned our bandit masks;
no shame among *Sai-yan*.
Our tartan wraps, Aran mufflers, lend a jaunty Tuareg air:
the Chinese know we're addled; a pair of crazy foreign devils.

Us? We're just friendly Marco Polos
searching out Li River Gorge to see famous weeping mountains
and read Li Bai, Tu Fu among craggy pines.

Breathing shallow, tracing out the last few scraps of oxygen—
How Long Can We Last?
Not a nick of open window, not a wisp of ventilation:

Consciousness is very low among the masses.

Our comrades feed us like monkeys at the zoo—apples, buns ...
The tea-man thumps his way toward us ceremonious in official apron,
flogging boiling water in huge Mongolian kettle-drum

Yam Cha! Yam Cha! Drink Tea!

(Ah, Dagda of the flaming Cauldron,
aren't ya the wise old Celt?
Cropping up among the mortal weak
with yer lifegiving cups;
a great pint-pot and a rinse of tea!
Praise be God and old-Golden Face, the Buddha.)

Hong Kong playboys of the semi-western world
and overseas Chinese flash smokes around:
      big face!
"Smoke?Marburrs... American."
Generous applause.
We truck on down the line.

      VI.

Canton's factories pass by; padi fields trim the horizon;
vegetable plots on every scrap of dirt,
bicycles everywhere.
Old men nod to maidens on the corners.

Bamboo and thatch
brick and steel, corrugated metal.
China out the window—
the dullest blocks of worker flats: Chinese
the meanest huts: Chinese
small gauge railway yards: Chinese.

The peasant beside my wife hacks noisily,
coughs a thick green lunger beside her boot;
we lift our bags to our knees
Gingerly.

"Jo-San! Hello! How you do?"

Smiling lady greets us with toothy grin.
An English teacher, village school;
are we enjoying China?
      You bet!
Says we should know about Chinese money,
and so buy tea whenever we like:
every *yuan* divided into tenths, then ten again
No sweat!

Drinking tea, breathing through face masks like third-rate movie
villains,
we watch China all about us;
no need for t.v. here,
it's happening before our eyes.
Smoking and smiling.

    VII.

We would sleep but there are No Berths.
Sit hardseat all the way? Enjoy the dining car instead—
chicken snak-paks, watery beer?
There are berths, of course;
Big Boss Conductor lounges soft in "All Full" compartment.
Thirty empty beds we count, a sleeping car "All Full"… reserved—
just in case
for, er, High Officials …

What to do?

This is Mother China;
3,000 years of civilization,
surely there is a way:
we are pilgrims, after all
though we knew there were no sleepers and chose to ride
Third Class, Hard-Seat among the masses.
In the absence of other choices we have made our bed
and now must lie not in it,
so to speak.

Ah, human nature.
We are weary, have money "at official rate."
A functionary stands before us in quiet dark of the blissful
sleeping car,
in baggy pantaloons he must deliver us to higher Authority.

So we return to Third Class, Hard-Seat, its blue-smoked masses
Drinking yet more tea
while bosses gain face at our expense
and we wait. What's another brutal hour among our brethren,
their peasant hardship,
forgiving them their rank humanity
and asking, silently
their forgiveness?

The boss will have his profit either way.
We get our berths;
money changes in the dark at costly foreign rate.

Big boss, with golden epaulets and golden smile
bids Sweet Dreams!

Tomorrow, Guilin, Li River Gorge:
China's immortal Mountains and Rivers
Without End at last,
hard rails behind us.

Tonight
adrift with open windows, fresh air and stars about,
we remember Wang Wei, Bai Juyi, the masterworks of Tang:
we are nearing our place/their exile.
This is all we have asked, travelling Third Class, Hard-Seat
among the masses.

Did Shirley McLaine see China this way
I wonder?

NEW CHINA, OLD WALLS SUITE

Beijing-Manchuria, 1998

I. *First Things In China*

Fields, people gotta eat;
cultivation everywhere like Great Plains only
more people.

So much tree planting;
one old walled compound, rough clay brick red
dotting landscape

FedEx jet sitting on airport runway.

II. *Sunday Morning*

7:20 am concert pianist, black gown arrives
Beijing Hotel Grand dining room.
Latin refrains
reverberate
far from home *Vaya condios*

Last night's rickshaw ramble through dusty hutongs—
alleys—a farewell
Vaya condios, Beijing.

III. *Edge of Town*

Edge of town, large tree planting operations
acacia, poplar, elm try keep down Gobi desert
dust.
The new 5 year plan places environment top priority;
air here like Mexico soup
eyes, throat burning.

Sheep graze among young trees.

IV. *For the Unknown Man Carrying His Mother Up the
Unbearable Hill On The Great Wall*

Too much burden for almost anyone;
through pilgrim crowds,
a figure, nestling ancient mother in arms, climbs
"the unbearable hill" at Great Wall, Badaling.

Here's China.
Did some critic talk about "the end of
suffering"?

New junk for sale.
Refurbished sites, newish brick here, there
along the Wall.
In town a massive city, Beijing
sprawls under reconstruction.

Old wall, new China.

New China. Old walls.

V. *Diplomacy*

Driving for hours in deep country on
mission to Zhuanghue;
setting off through rustbelt broken factories
railyards, smashed windows, curbs,
reconstruction everywhere; every brick recycled.
Vast workyards, mills, pedicab rag and bone men.
Manchuria/Manchester.

Transitions from city to rice fields:
Old grime, love of the colour red.
What is worn and ancient replaced with the less charming new.
Who wouldn't swap a fetid slum alley for a desert estate of
worker block tenements?
Better water, sewers, even in-door Turkish squats.

Over distance, beyond city, whole mountains carved
from forests, acacia bare,
ground to limestone—cement,
these slapdash high-rise towers. Faded and tawdry
near as soon built.

Then fields, the vegetable green of the country, and the driver
blaring Euro disco, 8:45 am.
Melons, treefarms, corn rows far as the eye can see.
Soon, brickyards, low kilns transmuting red earth to builder's clay,
village after non-descript village, low walls
tangle of rubble, cane, smoke.

Hour on hour,
through endless peasant China
mule-drawn ploughs,
unceasing peasant labour, hand-hoeing in fields,
stacking rock
tending orchards. Growing crops in every spare yard of land,
so many humans
so many mules
so many t.v. antennae.

Then there it is! Dusty Zhuanghue's new town sprawl.
Have the minstrels play "Open Up The Gates!"

VI.   *After Viewing the Shredder Plant*

Fog rolls in from the Bohai Sea covering
worker-bee towers,
cracked sidewalks, steps
bright showy tiny shopfronts up past
dogmeat restaurant.

Grind grind grind 'em up;
pare old bald tyres to shreds,
then grate shreds to asphalt dust.
Road scrap turning back to road
How we go on…
Pure Tao!

Machine produced at $1.2 million,
one-fifth U.S. price.
Please call GVRD back home
with urgent recycling news.

VII. *Long Black Cars*

Long black cars race down the road, pell-mell,
rockets of self-importance, warning lights flashing like tracers.

In the fields, farmers of thirty centuries stand in rows of corn, chest high,
straightening up, looking on as high officials race to the capitol.

Nothing new in three thousand years;
a puff of dust, no more:
only mandarins racing to the emperor's palace with all speed.

VIII. Special Economic Zone

Five hundred and fifty thousand new souls housed here
in less than fourteen years, built from scratch.
Dalian's northern oasis of high-rise business towers,
some lovely, most dull
a sprawling area—huge structures;
a booming economy for the millenium.

Here's the rub:
twenty-two story ghost blocks
concrete shells,
spectres of Asian financial meltdown,
unfinished and bankrupt,
here and there among the new;
victim of crony loans in Nippon, Korea,
Taiwan, take your pick.
Dead, grey as codfish.

It's Little Hong Kong here, same dormitories, upright tenements,
same energy, same dynamics, almost same clothes
just like Vancouver sometimes.

DESERT WALKING

I. *The Desert Variations*

Down the arroyo we spot the carcass, dog or goat, black one time
becoming sand, like at the River of Life and Death
in Katmandu.

Apaches—Mescaleros—lived here, Suzie says.
Peyote mescalero?
Button culture another way to the Big Paradise.

It's Eastertime. We're trying something different after Lent:
Prayer, breathing, desert walking, working at being kinder.

Farther up the canyon we find dry bones,
human maybe, bleached out in a rusting auto-wreck.
Nearby, there's a grove, shade trees planted in a circle
by druids unknown.
The only relief around.
Good place for building altars.

Our gifts are humble: these bones, a handful of cornflowers
and spent cartridges from near the creek.
Lots of mystery in the desert, Suzie says;
We don't come out too far here on our own.

Offering a prayer to Rattler and the desert gods,
we invoke their blessing on the bones
and take our leave.
Walking home, the silence hangs on both our tongues
while the desert wind blows up steady from the Mesa.

II. *Easter Sunday*

After searching four days,
finally on Easter morning in crossing
the arroyo and itching from desert scrub,
he shows in my field-glass lens,
        Western Meadowlark.

Alight on the naked branch,
breast puffed yellow and black
he stakes his claim with sagebrush matins
charming all the world.
It dawns upon me then:
no human sounds approach this nature's grace,
like a resurrection,
East Sunday in New Mexico.

                            Española
                            April 16/95

III. *At Taos*

In homage to his love of love
at D.H. Lawrence's shrine near Taos
we stop and read at 8,500 feet among the jack pines:
The Love Poems of Kenneth Patchen.
The San Cristobals loom snow-packed in the April
distance.

Back of the caretaker's place,
the meadow reaches off clear to Taos.
Three saddle mounts graze beneath strato-cumulus,
and a thin alpine wind licks at the last trace of snow.

In this simple chapel
once the poet's ashes laid.
We offer our Navajo feathers:
Great Lawrence is gone to Oneness;
the epic passions returned to aether.
Forehead pressed
to the cold draw of stone,
no single spirit still presides here, one can sense it.

This mulled quiet is knowingness enough.
Returning, we join with the fine, chill wind
that takes its course through the chaos of the world.

IV. *Airport Satori*

Standing in line, politely at airport
Albuquerque
this dusky woman with escort asks, What kind
of wood is your stick?
    Druid's wood. Me magick shillelagh. Maybe Malacca thorn.

Ohh. And the bone on the handle?

    Mountain Elk. The kneebone. Helluva doorknocker.

Did you hear that, Nanao?

Nanao Sakaki? Yes. Here in New Mexico we meet at last;
Nanao, from Japan
me down from Canada.
Sakaki, notorious wildman ninja renegade,
forever tromping through mountains like Dogen
watching wildlife.
Read his poems and weep and laugh at real Zen teishos.

Five years ago we met and worked through the mails,
and now, bound for Phoenix, we meet at last
flying friendly skies, with epic desert below
This faraway nearby moment
deep above Apache territory.

iv.17.95

V. *Suburban Music*

The mesas bloom in spattering April rain;
desert's another kind of paradise.

Birdlife bops oasis scrub lots:
grackles, doves, warblers, kingbirds.
A streamlined grebe cuts the air in back of Tempe Creek like a bullet.

Packing in a trucker's breakfast for the road again;
flasks of coffee, ham 'n eggs,
Key Lime pie.
The waitress with a Southern belle accent smiles
like crazy 'n says, I'm from right 'round here.

At Chandler, the din of migratory birds
leads up to hill country.
I turn, catch sight of Valley of the Sun,
laid out broad around Phoenix:
Pick a man off twenty miles distant in this
exceptional light;
and way off, Tucson a hundred miles to the south.

On a sunbake outcrop,
I track the Cactus Wrens that plug away
at huge Saguros down below.
Tea bush rustles in the afternoon wind;
dry scats litter flinty slopes among six kinds of cactus.

Desert sounds wilder than any aviary;
and the blooms erupt from old stones way beyond imagination,
swaying like diamond-backs.
The thought won't leave me:
tomorrow I head north for home.

As high as I can go this last Arizona day
I break beside a petroglyph, maybe Ute, on a black rock perch.
Ground squirrels yip incessant at my approach,
and I arrive in dodgey snake hollow then alert alert,
am shocked by a rapid strike at my face
Die, voyageur! King Rattler!

But no, breathe deep instead:
it's black-chinned hummingbird bidding
fond Farewell

Still alive!
So much thanks to give. So many species playing together like music.
Wild medicine:
this healing camp
called Desert.

VI. *Samarita*

The threads of old love dreams connect anew in hunger towns
flamenco rooms,
in rainstorms and lightning on the mount.

Their sketchy credentials rob the Muse of intellect
like tags of one-time ganga dreams,
small-breasted girls in wire-rim spectacles, Left Bank hair and
ragged bluejeans.
Her perfect feet.

Her lips glossed in the moonlight
like a sudden shower on saguro.
All day I watched lean cactus wrens,
unbeautiful, flit the wild hills.

She left for the city in pitch-black
talking God, the Buddha, the little death and sexual love.
I tossed in memory of our crossing the ocean
looking for a new country, new kicks, for a constant groove.
She told me it was the way of miracles
and I listened to the poetry of her blessing while her fingers
tapped a plaintive blues and Chet Baker's horn rubbed out sunrise.

If we had but world enough and time, then O wailing night,
O santana grit of dreams, there might truly be this
Only this,
If not, why not, or when—
in what other dream?

COYOTE SUNRISE

I.

The semi-trailers scream east like cyclones
out of the rising sun,
whirling dust that chokes your craw
hacking and gearing up for a new day on the
road.

Shuffling knapsack straps, I watch the big
rigs sluice across the valley plane,
disappearing off farmland horizon
miles away.

Across the road
commercial travellers spruce up in thirty
dollar rooms,
book early 'n stop by Denny's for fast
fuel and discourse on the
Presidential debate:
Did he win, or what!

Yarmulka cowboys, soldiers on furlough, teamsters in ballcaps
munch home-fries in presidential veneration.
Brownskin sweepers clean up tarmac beyond plate-glass windows,
and a copper woman slams her trunk to hit the
interstate for New Mexico.

When I took the ride
I reckoned him the silent type,
but he jived me on detective fictions,
sucking on a cola, heading for 'Frisco.

"So she screwed the bastard; took the cash,
torched the house, 'n him in it
and ran off with his pardner!
She broke the bank, broke his heart'n lowered the boom!
Cute 'n rich with her goddamned criminal lover
and her just a country gal…
So what does he say? What does he say now?
I'll tell ya:
'But God,' he says. 'God, she gave great head.'"

      II.

Davis, California: dry as dust.
Almond groves and rice checks gleaming hard
by power stations droning solitary
in this basket of the sun.
Threshers idling in vast, unwatered fields,
while in the foothills, flying low
a small green Cessna banks in metallic light.

Come dusk, sitting roadside thumbing and
pulling on a Coor's,
the manzanita and chapparal that once fed Indian goats
hums alive with chirping critters
the great, blue voice of night.

Above, honey-fed boys crash transmitters
on the moon,
tainting the last, pure vessel.

III.

My people saw the hand of God in sunlight,
knew His presence in the river's calm and tempests;
knew the awe and saw the wonder
in His commonwealth of stars.

Last night, sleeping in a cornfield
off the highway,
I heard the distant song of women calling down the
inner names of Q'uas,
Great Transformer
master of landscapes before the swirling
of Yin and Yang.

Life is a dream, they sang;
a silk cocoon the fates unwind at leisure
in these thorny lands
beneath the Milky Way.

The sun rises every morning:
we still believe these fictions, old Galileo.
The dharma-wheel turns slowly,
but change is sure.
And transformation comes,
a filament unnoticed in the absence of
final truths.

Life is a dream I heard them singing;
a dream we tread along uncertain paths,
that ends not with the dawn,
nor a darkening of the light
but in the hands of Q'uas,
a silent clap of thunder.

The lightning bolt of Buddha Mind.

THREE NEW YORK POEMS AS SONG

LEAVE-TAKING

At the departure gate
we kiss.
I say, Be Good.

She smiles,
whispers
Have Fun!

SELLING MANUSCRIPTS

West Sixth & Forty-Third
Outside the China Gift Shop,
a tiny sparrow
singing his heart out in the snow.

Life / in the heart / of Manhattan.

IN A STATION OF THE METRO

Lord, in my despair I looked upward,
and saw waterpipes,
florescent lights
the rusty crevices of worn-out tile.
The mosaic call of 42nd Street.

BINGLEY MOOR

I came to manhood in this landscape
tramping the dales, laying whole days
beneath Wordsworth skies; the Bronte ache
honed deep on Yorkshire's limestone stiles,
on the sheep skulls strewn on Bingley Moor.

Off narrow lanes
where Caedmon's shepherds lamented fallen angels,
black-eyed ewes heave in the mist
grunting a simple truth:
mud, filthy wool, mutton on the hoof.

Kindness is shaped by such hardness in the land;
joy came later in five pound flats
brooding on Milton for hours,
jazz crackling up from London
on the midnight wireless.

O love, you wandered all afternoon alone.
The brook you followed led to uncertain arms;
we sang without you at the inn.
Sadness is the rod of our teachings.
The brook ran fierce and spilled its course
among the rocks and moss of the trout pool
where we found you.

Now only memory parses what image still remains;
nights with pale lovers,
the flints one finds among fallen stiles,
or the frogs that leap in sunlight after flies
near the winter-blasted trees
on Bingley moor.

OLD MASTERS

About suffering they were never wrong…

W.H. Auden

Summer With Munch

These heuristic works, Edvard, beguile;
dispossessed, northern darkness everywhere.
Yet the lyric vein shows through like rainy weather
on the coast,
or snowy weather on the boulevards:

Jealousy Vampire The Kiss.

The evidence is overwhelming;
these sinewy burghers, their avaricious jaws of surfeit and darkness
are candidates for an *auto-da-fe*, Edvard;
tissues that fit us for the final melancholy.

The critics verdict is in progess.
Meanwhile, you thrust avuncular perspective into metabolic
diagnosis with this movie,
the grand pathetique, Edvard

    The Scream

    Madonna   The Hands

Hearing your new symphony, its colouratura movements
I would have called on you, Edvard, had you been here.
We might have walked a bit amid this chaos,
found matching bits of china in the pantry.
Even drunk our tea
with a real goblin.

WHAT JACK SHADBOLT SAID

Here's how he said *adios*
the last time we spoke:

"Art is experience given form.
I follow things expressively that interest me;
and try to express the experience of change that has happened to me.
My feeling now is that art is a matter of finding coherence, unity;
that deep down everyone wants to be an artist.
I feel if my experience is valid
it might also be valid for somebody else …

It's good to see you, boys."

MARIANNE FAITHFUL

Coarse and bawdy as Brecht & Weil
ever dreamed of,
barbed wire, thirty-five years of blues and fab.

"What is it that civilized humanity?
Bilbao moon…"

It ain't a travesty, but damn close to it;
it's just those mean ol' 20th Century Blues.
Here's a bit of real Berlin for the new millennium:
real decadence, over-ripe
slouching toward something like comfort for the meantime,
no ennui here—just the rats,
scurrying every which drunk-assed way
to be born again.

OLD MASTERS

Larkin and Robert Graves:
elder dogs about the fire, gone in a week.
Isherwood, Lizzie Smart, all gone;
all but the last of the last
classical generation.

Less competition, a wiseass says downtown.

As boys we played at Romans;
Tiberius and the rebellious slaves.
All Gaul divided in three before us,
we fenced with broadswords,
cursing in Latin.

From *Classics Illustrated* we moved on;
the Blues, Beats, then Yeats
and Eliot, Larkin and Graves—
the fare of older appetites
that grew to abiding love.

Farewell, Herr Ishvoo, unlocker of portals
from Berlin to the *Vedas*;
and Wild Lizzie of poems
and tales up the B.C. coast.
May the sun shine sweetly
on your bicycles, old mentors,
and on your eternal trampings
'round the sunny beaker of the golden South.
Sic transit gloria mundi.

The Blind Harper

Turlough O'Carolan, d. 1738, poet & minstrel;
greatest of the Irish harpers

O'Carolan
on your wanderings you passed no time
in the leaving of records.
I am your grandson though,
would know your histories,
the name and number of your days.

Your voice echoes in my heart, old bard
on reed and lyre,
in the shards you left behind:
gentle love songs, Celtic odes.
But the mist of years and shaming mind,
the crows of time,
erased the favour of your riotous name;
and now, your own blood
knows nothing of you.

Grandfather,
in those great halls that welcomed you
betimes upon the open road
did you never cast an eye beyond the sun?
The music of the spheres has claimed yours
for its own.
O, that you had left some sign
or word.

FORTY-NINTH DAY

for Evalina Kats, in memoriam

The dusk is alive with birdsong:
purple finch, chickadee.
Late August rain drips and bounces in
lime-green thickets,
where already, the old apple sheds her first
falling leaves.

In the stillness of falling light
the incense drifts, drawn upward to blue-grey
skies:

The essence of self returning to all component
non-self elements.

Higher up the slope,
a pair of towering hemlock pierces the ether as
clouds settle on the ridge:

Heaven's breath touching Earth;
Gaia's hands embracing the mystery.

What it is, is this—
our common prayer:
a burning stick, a *Book of Hours*,
the wavering of a spotless flower in fading light:

The river runs,
The blossom's fragrance drifts above the void.

Notes on the Poems

Deep Cove

p. 17, *Kul-shan*: Salish, popularly known as Mount Baker.

p. 20, *Gatha*: brief Buddhist prayer of mindfulness

p. 22, The 8th cent. scholar Alcuin gave Europe its first popular hand-written script—Carolingian Miniscule. In 1988, Celtic scholar Rudi Diesvelt made a pilgrimage in his honour.

p. 23, Big Whiskers: local Burrard Inlet children's term for harbour seals. In 1995, the author published an environmental mystery book for young-sters, entitled *Big Whiskers Saves The Cove* (Concorde Books).

p. 25, Larry Lillo: acclaimed as one of Canada's most innovative theatre producers, died of AIDS in 1993.

The Calgary Suite

Poems were inspired during a two year residence (1986-88). Moving in time and space from B.C.'s gulf islands, through the Cariboo country, to Calgary's Bow River Valley, they pay homage to the tradition of a work-ing man leaving home and family in search of work. *The Calgary Suite*, with poems as text, has been performed widely with composer/pianist Mark Armanini and an ensemble of Canadian musicians.

"Jackson's Ranch, Cache Creek, 1948." This work by prairie artist Illingworth Kerr at Calgary's Glenbow Museum was a frequent source of inspiration.

The Music of the Stones

A commissioned suite of poems/texts. It follows a westerner's pilgrimage along Asia's dharma trail in search of enlightenment and ends in North Vancouver.

p. 48, *Machhapuchare*: the spectacular 21,000 ft. fish-tail Himalayan peak above Pokhara, Nepal. Kumari is the living goddess, chosen at about age five, venerated by Nepalis at Katmandu's Durbar Square until puberty, when she is replaced.

p. 50, *Pagan*: site of a once fabulous city-state in Burma. Founded by King Anarudha in 1057 A.D, it was ransacked by Kublai Khan in 1287 and never rebuilt. Much of its history remains unknown. Thatbyinnyu is the highest of its 5,000 pagodas.

p. 53, *Daruma*: Japanese form of Bodhidharma, bringer of Dhyana/ Zen meditation to China, approx. 600 AD.

p. 55, Stylized phrases are movements of Tai Chi Chuan.

p.57, A transliteration from the Chinese of Taoist Master Loy Ching-Yuen.

Gathering Stones

p. 67, Leonard Peltier: American Indian activist, accused of murder at Wounded Knee, fled to Canada seeking sanctuary. Captured, he was extradited to the U.S., 1975-76 and is still imprisoned.

p. 72, *Eightfold Path*: the fourth Noble Truth of the Buddha's core teaching, offering a basic program of guidance.

Celtic Highway

p. 88, In a moment of great self-doubt, Sumo master O'Nami was urged by his mentor to meditate upon the nature of ocean waves. Thus inspired, he became an invincible champion.

p. 91, *Ad astra per aspera*: "to the stars by hard means."

p. 94, *Sai-yan*: westerners

p. 95, *Yam-cha*: "drinking tea." The reference to Dagda of the Flaming Cauldron is Irish, from the pantheon of Celtic gods.

p. 99, *New China, Old Walls Suite*: References are drawn from the author's trade mission to Beijing and Manchuria in June 1998.

The Gaelic of the Afterword, *laithean a dh'aom* translates roughly as "the days that have passed," or perhaps *Auld Lang Syne*. *Slainte*, Irish greeting and drinking toast.

For good medicine, thanks to Muddy Waters & Otis Spann, Abel Bello & Marcos Yrizarry, Darshan Singh, T.S. Selvarajah, Josh Grundy, Eric Hunter, Alan Watts, Henry Miller, David Watmough, Kiki, Nina Simone, Lachlin Loud, Rudi & Gretchen Diesvelt, Henry Young, and all the clan.

Laithean a dh'aom
Slainte

About the Author

Trevor Carolan teaches English and Asian Religion at University College of the Fraser Valley. He is married with two children and lives in North Vancouver, British Columbia where he served for three years as an elected municipal councillor. His travel novel *The Pillow Book of Dr. Jazz* is published by Anchor. He is also the author of *Giving Up Poetry: With Allen Ginsberg At Hollyhock*, a memoir of his acquaintance with the beloved late poet (Banff Centre Press). He is a frequent contributor to *The Bloomsbury Review* and *Shambhala Sun* magazine.